U.S. ARMY by the Numbers

by Lisa M. Bolt Simons

Consultant: Major (Ret.) Margaret Griffin, MS
U.S. Army
Atlanta, Georgia

CAPSTONE PRESS
a capstone imprint

Edge Books are published by Capstone Press,
1710 Roe Crest Drive, North Mankato, Minnesota 56003
www.capstonepub.com

Library of Congress Cataloging-in-Publication Data
Simons, Lisa M. B., 1969–
  U.S. Army by the numbers / by Lisa M. Bolt Simons.
    pages cm. — (Edge. Military by the numbers.)
  Includes bibliographical references and index.
  Summary: "Describes aspects of the U.S. Army using numbers, stats, and info
graphics"— Provided by publisher.
  Audience: Grades 4 to 6.
  ISBN 978-1-4765-3917-1 (library binding)
  ISBN 978-1-4765-5120-3 (paperback)
  ISBN 978-1-4765-5965-0 (ebook PDF)
1. United States. Army—Juvenile literature. I. Title.
UA25.S5712 2014
355.00973—dc23   2013032521

Editorial Credits
Mandy Robbins and Brenda Haugen, editors
Heidi Thompson, designer
Danielle Ceminsky, production specialist

Photo Credits
Alamy: Lightroom Photos, 14; DoD photo by Spc. De'Yonte Mosley, U.S. Army, 21 (top); Getty
Images: Robert Nickelsberg, 19 (left), Time Life Pictures/David Scherman, 16; Library of
Congress, 9; Shutterstock: Vartanov Anatoly, 6 (M9); U.S. Air Force photo by SSgt. Aaron D.
Allmon II, 6 (M120), Staff Sgt. Angelita M. Lawrence, 26-27, Tech Sgt. Francisco V. Govea II, 24
(top left), Tech. Sgt. Sean M. Worrell, 17; U.S. Army photo, 5, 19 (right), 20 (left), 24 (bottom),
25 (left), Sgt. Kimberly Lamb, 6 (MK19-3), Sgt. Heather Denby, 25 (right), Sgt. Igor Paustovski,
18, Sgt. John Crosby, 6-7, Sgt. Kissta DiGregorio, 21 (middle), Sgt. Maj. Rich Greene, 21 (bottom
left), Spc. Gregory Gieske, 6 (M109A6), Staff Sgt. James Allen, 21 (bottom right), Staff Sgt. Jason
Epperson, 12-13, Staff Sgt. Kevin L. Moses Sr, 20 (right), Staff Sgt. Teddy Wade, 8; U.S. Coast
Guard photo by Chief Photographer's Mate Robert F. Sargent, 22-23; U.S. Marine Corps photo, 6
(M224), Lance Cpl. Angela Hitchcock, 10-11; U.S. Navy photo by Ensign Haraz Ghanbari, cover,
1, MC1 Thomas Coffman, 24 (top right); Wikipedia/PEOSoldier, 6 (M24A3)

Design Elements
Shutterstock: Adrian Grosu, Aleksandar Mijatovic, Oleg Zabielin, URRRA, Yaraz

Printed in the United States of America in Stevens Point, Wisconsin
092013   007768WZS14

Table of Contents

America's Soldiers

For more than 200 years, soldiers in the United States Army have protected their nation. Soldiers train their bodies and minds to perform well, even in life-threatening conditions. From weaponry to what a recruit needs for basic training, this is the Army—by the numbers.

The Soldiers

489,000

677,000+ Soldiers

/89,000

Active duty (72%)

Army Reserve (28%)

officers (17%)   enlisted (83%)

15% female

85% male

$2,199.90
monthly base pay earned

4 years: average service

Number of Soldiers

9–10	16–44	62–190	300–1,000	3,000–5,000	10,000–15,000	20,000–45,000

Soldier Units

squad

platoon

company

battalion

brigade

division

corps

Medal of Honor Army Recipients

War	Recipients
Civil War (1861–1865)	1,198
American Indian Campaigns (1790–1891)	426
World War I (1914–1918)	95
World War II (1939–1945)	324
Korean War (1950–1953)	82
Vietnam War (1959–1975)	161
Operation Iraqi Freedom (2003–2011)	4
Operation Enduring Freedom–Afghanistan (2001–)	4

Army Weapons

WEAPON		WEIGHT
M9 pistol		(loaded) **2.6 lb**
M24A3 sniper rifle		(loaded) **18.3 lb**
MK19-3 40 mm Grenade Machine Gun		**72.4 lb**
M224 Mortar (conventional)		**48 lb**
M120/M121 Mortar		**319 lb**
M109A6 Paladin		(combat ready) **63,615 lb**

AMMO	RANGE
15 rounds	**50 meters**
5 rounds	**1.2 km**
up to **375 rounds** per minute	**2.2 km**
18-30 rounds per minute for 1-4 minutes	**3.5 km**
16 rounds for first minute, then 4 rounds per minute	**7.2 km**
4 rounds per minute for first 3 minutes, then 1 round per minute	**30 km**

The Army in 3s

3 phases in the Army's Basic Combat Training (BCT): Red, White, and Blue

3 pairs of white underwear to bring to BCT

13 Army job code number for anything to do with Field Artillery; specific numbers and letters are assigned to each Military Occupational Specialty (MOS).

30 number of soldiers in a platoon that carries 400 pounds of batteries to power equipment during a 3-day mission

+

33 number of combat-equipped soldiers that can be carried in a Boeing CH-47 Chinook, the Army's largest helicopter

103 number of years after his time in combat when President Theodore Roosevelt was awarded the Medal of Honor

3,000+ rounds in a 7.62 mm machine gun on a Stryker MGS vehicle

362,015 number of soldiers serving in the Army National Guard in 2010

$30,000 maximum bonus for a 3-year enlistment

The Abrams Tank

No vehicle is more identified with the United States Army than the Abrams tank. This tank provides soldiers with mobility, protection, and firepower.

1980 entered United States service

Top Speed
41.5 miles per hour

Width
12 feet

Height
8 feet

Length
32 feet

Weapons on M1A1

120 mm XM256 smooth bore cannon

.50 caliber M2 machine gun

Ammunition Storage

- 42 rounds—120 mm gun
- 11,400 rounds—7.62 mm gun
- 900 rounds—.50 caliber gun
- 32 screening grenades

Weight
67.6 tons

A Ready Soldier

$5,000+

the average value of equipment and clothing for each soldier

Soldiers are issued their general gear at BCT. Once they arrive at their post, they must check in at the Central Issue Facility (CIF). This is where they receive gear and clothing that is specific to their unit or geographic location. Depending on the weather at the post and the type of mission, some of what is issued varies. Ammunition, chemical protection, and other gear is provided later and varies according to the mission.

1 advanced combat helmet (ACH)

1 ATN PVS7-2 Night Vision Goggles (NVGs)

1 Ghillie Suit—camouflage that has artificial vegetation on it for better concealment

1 M16 rifle

2 first-aid kits

4 uniforms

2 Army Combat Uniforms (ACU) with camouflage pattern

2 ACUs with fire resistance

1 set of body armor

1 vest

4 protective and ballistic inserts

8 tan T-shirts

1 M40 series gas mask

4 choices of water container; all have a tube that can be used with a gas mask

4 pairs of underwear (male soldiers)

0 undergarments (female soldiers–self-equipped)

1 Joint Service Lightweight Integrated Suit Technology (JSLIST) for chemical protection

Battle of the Bulge, World War II

The Battle of the Bulge is considered one of the largest and bloodiest battles of World War II. German dictator Adolf Hitler wanted to break apart the American and British forces stationed in Europe. In the winter of 1944, he ordered a surprise attack in the forests of northwest Europe. The German soldiers pushed through the **Allied forces** and formed a bulge in the Allied lines. But the Allies fought back and eventually pushed the Germans back. The U.S. Army was a major force in the victory.

16 December 16, 1944: the day the Germans attacked

3 weeks the battle lasted

75 mile stretch of the Ardennes Forest, dense woods with few roads where four American divisions were resting

Allied forces—a group of countries including the United States, England, and France that fought together in World War II

about
600,000
American soldiers fighting

1 word spoken when the acting commander of the U.S. 101st Airborne Division was told to surrender. He said, "Nuts!" and refused.

500 pounds: weight of the bomb that killed 30 wounded U.S. soldiers along with nurse Renee Lemaire on December 24, 1944, at an American Aid Station

about
200,000
German troops

80,000
approximate number of American soldiers killed, wounded, or captured

100,000
approximate number of Germans killed, wounded, or captured

3 times U.S. General Omar Bradley had to prove his identity. He did this by answering questions about American football and actress Betty Grable. U.S. soldiers were forced to prove their identities after some English-speaking Germans had impersonated U.S. soldiers.

15

Then and Now

1949

Soldier's average monthly pay:

enlisted Private/less than 4 months of service:

$75

Colonel/less than 2 years of service:

$570

General/less than 2 years of service:

$926

new house: **$7,450**

new car: **$1,420**

gallon of gas: **$0.17**

2013

Soldier's average monthly pay:

enlisted Private/less than
4 months of service:

$1,402

Colonel/less than
2 years of service:

$6,064

General/less than
2 years of service:

$14,975

new house: **$200,000**

new car: **$30,000**

gallon of gas: **$3.38**

Operation Iraqi Freedom

On March 17, 2003, President George W. Bush demanded that Iraqi dictator Saddam Hussein and his sons leave Iraq within 48 hours. They had committed criminal acts against Iraqis and neighboring countries. President Bush also believed Hussein had weapons of mass destruction. Hussein didn't leave the country. The U.S. invasion of Iraq began on March 20, 2003. The six-week invasion turned into an eight and a half-year war that officially ended in 2011.

170,000+ U.S. troops stationed in Iraq at more than 500 bases at the peak of the war

1,500,000+ Americans served in Iraq

6,000,000+ miles an Army transportation battalion recorded during about 300 **convoys**, supplying 20 bases in Iraq

32,226 Americans wounded

4,487 Americans died

nearly **9,000** awards given to soldiers for bravery

$1,694,700,000,000 cost of the Iraq war and war-related expenses

convoy—group of vehicles traveling together, usually in single file and accompanied by armed forces

32

U.S. Army Apache helicopters searched for 40,000 Iraqi Republican Guard troops hidden south of Baghdad.

March 23, 2003

April 9, 2003

December 13, 2003

39 feet

height of the Saddam Hussein statue that was pulled down by Iraqi men and U.S. troops

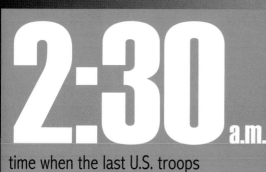

2:30 a.m.

time when the last U.S. troops started to secretly leave Iraq

8 feet

depth of the hole in which Saddam Hussein was hiding when

Working in the Army

The Army has more than 150 jobs to choose from, from fighting on the front lines to playing in a military band. Special tests help identify career options for recruits.

- detects mines
- basic **demolition**
- builds bridges
- makes obstacles

14 WEEKS OF TRAINING

Combat Engineer

main combat forces on the ground; may lead to advanced training such as sniper or airborne school

14 WEEKS OF TRAINING

Infantry

demolition—the act of destroying something

5 FUNCTIONS

1. support operations
2. site security
3. law and order
4. military prisoners
5. intelligence

Military Police

47 specialties from allergies to heart surgery

provides health care to soldiers and their families

Medical Corps

1 language other than English that recruits learn to understand fluently

1 qualification for top secret clearance needed to go to training

20 WEEKS OF ADVANCED TRAINING

27 CAREER OPTIONS

keeps vehicles and machines working, from medical equipment to missile systems

 **Mechanic**

Human Intelligence Collector

D-Day

"D-Day" refers to the first day of the Normandy Invasion during World War II. This two-month-long battle began to free western Europe from the grip of Nazi Germany. It was a turning point in the war, and the U.S. Army played a major role.

June 6, 1944
invasion

160,000
Allied troops landed along the beaches

55 number of divisions of soldiers the Germans had in France

133,000+ soldiers began the march across Europe to defeat the Germans

12 Medal of Honor recipients

19 U.S. Army divisions

5 beach code names
   Utah
   Omaha
   Gold
   Juno
   Sword

By June 30, 1944, the following had landed on the Normandy shores:

850,000+ men
148,000 vehicles
570,000 tons of supplies

4,000 to 9,000 German soldiers killed or wounded

50 number of miles of Normandy coastline where the Allied troops landed

13,000+ Allied parachute troopers jumped behind enemy lines five hours before the attack on the beach.

10,300+ Allied soldiers killed or wounded

K-9s

Dogs serve alongside human soldiers in the U.S. Army. The K-9 Corps provides protection and support in peacetime and during battles.

March 1942

The K-9 Corps was established.

18,000 dogs went to training centers when program began

8,000 dogs failed initial exams

8 weeks training, minimum; 12 weeks, maximum

4 specialties—**sentry**, scout or patrol, messenger, or mine dog

15 war dog platoons established, seven in Europe and eight in the Pacific

sentry—a guard

Standout Canine Soldiers

Sgt. Stubby

Chips

Sgt. Stubby, a pit bull, survived 17 battles during World War I. He was the first dog to be given a rank in the military after he captured a German spy. Stubby also alerted soldiers to gas attacks and survived a grenade attack.

Chips was a German Shepherd mix that served in the 3rd Infantry Division in World War II. Chips attacked enemy gunmen to allow U.S. troops who were trapped on a beach in Italy to escape. For his bravery Chips received the Distinguished Service Cross, Silver Star, and Purple Heart. The awards were later taken back because he wasn't human.

32 breeds initially accepted

7 breeds currently allowed—German Shepherds, Belgian sheepdogs, Doberman Pinschers, collies, Siberian huskies, Malamutes, and Eskimo dogs

The Army in 1s

To bring to Basic
Combat Training (BCT)

1
- **pair of white, calf-high, athletic socks**
- **pair of comfortable shoes**
- **day's worth of clothes**
- **combination lock or padlock**

100 hours (about four days) of Operation Desert Storm (Persian Gulf War) in January 1991

10 weeks of BCT

$100 cash in excess of $100 is unauthorized at Ranger School and could get a soldier kicked out

1,000 approximate number of gallons of fuel a Chinook helicopter holds

100+ miles per hour: speed a Silver Wings parachute jumper reaches during two miles of free fall

$1,000,000 cost of ammunition used in training in 2013

Special Operations Forces

Soldiers in the U.S. Army Special Operations Forces (SOF) are highly trained. The Army SOF includes different groups. Each group performs specialized, dangerous missions.

Army Special Forces: elite soldiers whose missions include special reconnaissance and counterterrorism; commonly referred to as Green Berets

40% of soldiers who are assessed for Army Special Forces are successful and move on to the next phases of training.

5 phases of training

3 words **De Oppresso Liber** meaning "To Liberate the Oppressed," the motto of the Army Special Forces

4 Army Special Forces specialties
- weapons
- engineering
- communications
- medical

1961 first green beret hats are given to the Army Special Forces by President John F. Kennedy

reconnaissance—a mission to gather information about an enemy
counterterrorism—actions taken against terrorism; terrorism is the use of violence and destructive acts to create fear and to achieve a political or religious goal

160th Special Operations Aviation Regiment (SOAR):

This SOF provides helicopter support for military operations that are usually performed at night. SOAR members are commonly called Night Stalkers.

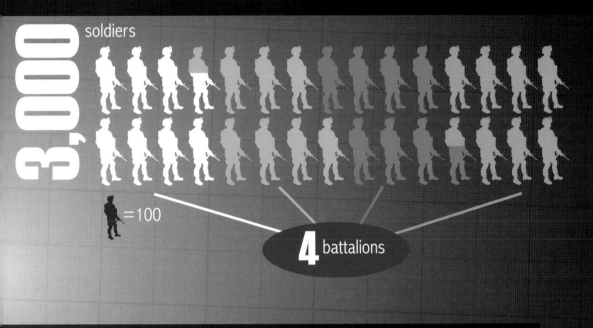

3,000 soldiers

 =100

4 battalions

Rangers: soldiers who specialize in direct-action raids, such as air assault, facility destruction, and the capture of enemies

52 Military Occupational Specialties (MOS) or jobs in the 75th Ranger Regiment

8 weeks of training for enlisted soldiers at the Ranger Assessment and Selection Program (RASP 1)

3 weeks of training for officers (RASP 2)

5 parts of the Ranger philosophy

1. physical fitness
2. marksmanship
3. medical training
4. mobility
5. small unit tactics

Glossary

Allied forces (AL-lyd FOR-suhss)—countries united against Germany, Italy, and Japan during World War II, including France, the United States, Canada, and Great Britain

ballistic (buh-LIS-tik)—having to do with the science and study of bullets and missiles

convoy (KAHN-voi)—group of vehicles traveling together, usually accompanied by armed forces

counterterrorism (KOUN-tur TER-ur-i-zuhm)—actions taken against terrorism; terrorism is the use violence and destructive acts to create fear and to achieve a political or religious goal

demolition (de-muh-LI-shuhn)—the act of destroying something

dictator (DIK-tay-tuhr)—someone who has complete control of a country, often ruling it unjustly

post (POHST)—a military base where soldiers are stationed or trained

reconnaissance (ree-KAH-nuh-suhnss)—a mission to gather information about an enemy

round (ROUND)—one shot fired by a weapon

sentry (SEN-tree)—a guard

Read More

Delmar, Pete. *The U.S. Army Green Berets: The Missions*. American Special Ops. North Mankato, Minn.: Capstone Press, 2014.

Goldish, Meish. *Army: Civilian to Soldier*. Becoming a Soldier. New York: Bearport Pub., 2011.

Hamilton, John. *United States Army*. United States Armed Forces. Edina, Minn.: ABDO Pub., 2012.

Internet Sites

FactHound offers a safe, fun way to find Internet sites related to this book. All of the sites on FactHound have been researched by our staff.

Here's all you do:

Visit *www.facthound.com*

Type in this code: 9781476539171

Check out projects, games and lots more at
www.capstonekids.com

Index

Titles in this set:

U.S. AIR FORCE by the **Numbers**

U.S. MARINES by the **Numbers**

U.S. ARMY by the **Numbers**

U.S. NAVY by the **Numbers**